BLACKBIRD

Adam Rapp

BROADWAY PLAY PUBLISHING INC
224 E 62nd St, NY NY 10065-8201
212 772-8334 fax: 212 772-8358
BroadwayPlayPubl.com

BLACKBIRD
© Copyright 2004 by Adam Rapp

First printing: November 2004
This printing: November 2011
I S B N: 978-0-88145-249-5

Book design: Marie Donovan
Typeface: Palatino
Printed and bound in the U S A

BLACKBIRD originally received a workshop production at Mabou Mines in their 2000 Artist Suite Residency with the following cast and creative contributors:

BAYLIS ....Shannon Parr
FROGGY .... Elizabeth Reaser

Director .... Adam Rapp
Set & lighting design .... Jane Cox
Costume design ....Rebecca Dowd
Sound design .... Eric Shim
Production stage manager .... Nick Mickozzi

Mentor .... Lee Breuer

BLACKBIRD received its world premiere at the Bush Theatre in London, England, on 8 June 2001. The cast and creative contributors were:

BAYLIS .... Paul Sparks
FROGGY .... Elizabeth Reaser

Director ....Mike Bradwell
Set & costume design .... Lisa Lillywhite
Lighting design .... Tanya Burns
Sound design ....Paul Bull
Production stage manager .... Zoe Cupit

This revised version of BLACKBIRD was produced in off-Broadway by Edge Theater Company at the Blue Heron Arts Center. The cast and creative contributors were:

BAYLIS .... Paul Sparks
FROGGY .... .Mandy Siegfried

Director .... .Adam Rapp
Set design .... David Korins
Costume design .... Victoria Farrell
Lighting design .... .Jane Cox
Sound design .... Eric Shim
Production stage manager .... Sarah Izzo

CHARACTERS & SETTING

BAYLIS, *early thirties, an angry young man*
FROGGY, *ninteen, a young woman*

Time: Christmas Eve, the late nineties

Place: a rented room on Canal Street, New York City

ACT ONE

(Smog's You Moved In *plays while lights fade up on a room on Canal Street. The song fades when the lights reach their full intensity.)*

(A desk. An orphaned chair. Next to the desk, a garbage can. A makeshift, egg crate mattress on the floor, scraps of paper peaking out here and there. Next to the mattress, an old golf bag riddled with rock-n-roll stickers and various forms of personal graffiti. In a pocket of the golf bag a dented lunchbox. Downstage right, a closet. An old factory window upstage left. Strips of electric tape pasted over a few cracks in the window pane. Neon light blinking on the window. Along the stage left wall, an old iron radiator. Attached to the radiator piping are a series of bike chains. At the end of the chains there is a pair of old police handcuffs. Scattered about are several empty bottles of Jack Daniels. In one corner a garbage can with debris around its base. On the desk a phone, an ashtray choked with cigarette butts, a bottle of Jack Daniels with a Christmas bow tied around the neck, a hard-bound dictionary whose spine is reinforced with duct tape, a few paperback novels, a cheap radio, a few cans of Sterno, a few rolls of toilet paper and a used manual typewriter. On top of the radio, an Altoids box. The phone line snakes across the floor and out the front door. Used tissues scattered everywhere.)

(Under the desk a picnic cooler and an unplugged, kicked-in T V with aluminum foil sculpted over the antenna.)

(BAYLIS, *thirty-two, is smoking at the desk, listening to
Christmas jazz on the radio. He wears sweatpants, an old
T-shirt, and a cheap housecoat. On his feet he wears one black
sock and his other foot is bandaged with gauze and black
electric tape.*)

(*Wreaths of cigarette smoke hover in the room. Around the
desk it appears as if his whole life has been organized within
arm's reach: clothes, books, food items, boxes of things here
and there. Throughout the course of the play he uses a
pinch-end stick grapper, much like the ones seen in corner
delis. There is the sense that he has been there for a very long
time.*)

BAYLIS: You comin out or what? (*He looks to the closet,
smokes.*) Can't hide in there all night, Froggy. Ain't
enough air. Oxygen burns up faster than you think.
You'll be breathin monoxide in a few. (*He smokes.*)
At least crack the damn door, make me feel better.

(*The closet door is opened a sliver. After a moment there is a
single knock from the inside of the closet.*)

BAYLIS: Come on out of there now. I said I wouldn't hit
you. (*He scans the dial on the radio, finds Christmas music.*)
Listen to that. Silent Night right on cue. You know that
part of the song where they sing 'round young virgin,
mother and child'? I used to think they were singin
proud conversion. Proud conversion, mother and child.
What the fuck's a proud conversion, anyway? Come
sing a song with me, Froggy. (*He grabs the dictionary,
starts thumbing through it.*) I don't know how you can
stand it in there. My laundry's all over the place.
Underwear. Towels. Goddamn sweatsocks.

(*Four knocks from the inside of the closet*)

BAYLIS: Gonna leave me out here all alone on Christmas
Eve? (*He breaks the seal on a bottle of whiskey, takes a nip.*)
I'll miss you, Froggy.

(Three knocks from the inside of the closet)

BAYLIS: I'm sorry, okay? That what you wanna hear?
I'm sick with sorrow. I got sorrow in my nose. I got
sorrow in my gums. I got sorrow down my pants.
There's so much sorrow I don't even know what to
do with it. Look, there's sorrow coming outta my
goddamn anus.

(The closet door opens slowly and FROGGY, *a nineteen-year-old girl steps out. There is a bruise on her forehead. She is
small for her age and bundled in layers of T-shirts and
thermals. She wears a large knit hat nearly pulled over her
eyes. There is a lost, hidden beauty about her. The layers give
her the air of an adolescent boy who is about to go play in a
snowdrift. She goes for the Altoids box.* BAYLIS *intercepts.
She unplugs the radio, pissed, then crosses to the window.)*

FROGGY: I tap out codes but you don't get em.

BAYLIS: I get em. You don't think I get em?

FROGGY: I tap three times but you don't know what I
say. One four and three.

BAYLIS: I heard you tappin, Froggy.

FROGGY: You wouldn't know the code if it hit you in
the dick.

BAYLIS: What the hell do you know about what I know
and what I don't know? Take your hat off, I can't even
see you.

FROGGY: You think I don't get stuff but I get stuff. Just
cause you know words don't make you special.

BAYLIS: Hey, I don't know shit. Goddamn *squat's* what I
know. If I knew something I wouldn't be penned up in
this room like a fuckin pig.

FROGGY: If you were an animal that's what you'd be.

BAYLIS: What, a pig?

FROGGY: A pig with a big hairy ass.

BAYLIS: And what would you be, a goddamn peacock?

FROGGY: I wouldn't be no animal.

BAYLIS: Oh yeah? What would you be, a car? A fuckin rowboat?

FROGGY: I'd be a plant.

BAYLIS: A plant?!

FROGGY: I'd be green. Like grass or lettuce.

BAYLIS: You'd prolly be one of them big horny-ass jungle bushes. One of them abadaba plants that'll swallow a dog.

FROGGY: Or I'd be some snow. That's what I'd be, I'd be snow.

BAYLIS: You'd be a little wildcat is what you'd be, Froggy.

FROGGY: You don't know.

BAYLIS: Yes I do know. You'd be a little fang-toothed, crooked-tailed wildcat.

FROGGY: You're just sayin that cause you want some pussy, Fuckface.

BAYLIS: Pussy?

FROGGY: You think it'll get me goin. You can screw that radio for all I care.

BAYLIS: You're just mad.

FROGGY: No I ain't.

BAYLIS: I was just teasin you. Take your hat off, you're gonna start a goddamn fire in here.

FROGGY: You spell it.

BAYLIS: Spell what.

FROGGY: That word.

BAYLIS: What word.

FROGGY: That big word with all the parts in it.

BAYLIS: Cars have parts. Words have syllables.

FROGGY: Whatever, Dickless. Spell it.

BAYLIS: Now you know I can spell it, Froggy. I used to win bets on that word.

FROGGY: Do it then, bitch.

BAYLIS: Why you gotta be so goddamn stubborn?

FROGGY: I ain't stubborn.

BAYLIS: Yes you are. You're stubborner than a fuckin rope.

FROGGY: If you had a dick you'd spell it, Baylis.

BAYLIS: Hey, that's the first time you said my name in four damn days. I was startin to think I was Dickless. Or Fuckface. *(He hands her the dictionary, points to a spot, turns.)* Antidisestablishmentarianism. A-N-T-I-D-I-S-E-S-T-A-B-L-I-S-H-M-E-N-T-A-R-I-A-N-I-S-M. Antidisestablishmentarianism.

FROGGY: What does it mean?

BAYLIS: It's a fuckin noun and it means 'opposition to the withdrawal of state support or recognition from an established church, especially the Anglican church in Nineteenth-Century England.' It also means I win you lose get me a beer.

(He turns back to the desk. She crosses to the desk with the dictionary, drops it in the trash. She then reaches into the cooler, sets a beer in front of him.)

FROGGY: I could be snow, Dickless, I could. I know I could be snow. The parts of it. Like the flakes. The way they look on T V. All white and stuff. All white like a cake. Snow don't really have much to do, if you think about it. Not much to do but fall. Fall all quiet and relaxed and stuff.

BAYLIS: Take your goddamn clothes off, you're givin me a fever.

(She takes her hat off. She peels off her many shirts, one layer after the other, until she starts to remove the final T-shirt.)

BAYLIS: Keep that one on. I don't want to see your tits.

(She puts the T-shirt back on, starts to take her pants down.)

BAYLIS: Keep your pants on, too. I'm tired of lookin at those bruises on your knees.

(She pulls her pants back up.)

BAYLIS: Lemme feel you.

(She steps up to him without hesitation, sits on his lap. He puts his hand down her pants.)

FROGGY: If I was snow I'd live on a mountain with goats and stuff. Goats and beavers and snakes. They'd try to piss on me but I'd yell at them cause snow's got a voice. You can't hear it, but it's there like a whisper. It hides in the cloud puffs. There's this song about a snowman who melts into a puddle. I could be that, too. I could be a puddle.

(He stops feeling her.)

BAYLIS: How come you don't do nothin when I touch you like that?

FROGGY: I do stuff.

BAYLIS: No you don't. I was strokin you up and you weren't doin a damn thing.

FROGGY: I was talkin.

BAYLIS: Don't you feel nothin?

FROGGY: I feel your hand.

BAYLIS: Well, what's it like?

FROGGY: I don't know. A hand.

BAYLIS: You used to feel more than that.

FROGGY: A hand with bones and skin.

(She goes for something in his shirt pocket. He catches her hand, squeezes it, puts her to the floor, twisting her arm.)

BAYLIS: Or at least you acted like you felt more than that! You don't even get wet no more, do you? Dry as a goddamn sandbox.

(He releases her arm.)

FROGGY: Spit in it if you want it wet.

BAYLIS: *(Pointing in her face)* I'll spit somewhere all right. Spit right in your eye.

FROGGY: I can smell your anus on your hand, Fuckface. Like monkeys at the zoo. What'd you do, poop your pants again?

BAYLIS: Watch it.

FROGGY: *(Mocking)* Watch it.

BAYLIS: I ain't in the mood.

FROGGY: *I* ain't in the mood.

(BAYLIS smells his hand, wheels over to the trash, pulls out the dictionary, plugs in the radio. FROGGY crosses to the window, peers out, starts to fidget and scratch her arms.)

BAYLIS: You used to make me fight for it. And you'd get wet as a waterslide. Now you just walk right over and give it to me all parched and shit. What the fuck is that about?

FROGGY: I wanna do some heroin. Gimme some heroin, Baylis.

BAYLIS: You only got a little left.

FROGGY: What else is there?

BAYLIS: All I got's the China White and some of that
liquid Novocain Murl stole from his dentist.

FROGGY: What's the Novocain do?

BAYLIS: It numbs you.

FROGGY: Can you drink it?

BAYLIS: You shoot it. Dentists use it when they drill
your teeth and shit. I'm savin it.

FROGGY: Savin it for what?

BAYLIS: Pasta sauce. Hell, I don't know.

FROGGY: What about that Blackfoot in the closet?

BAYLIS: That Blackfoot's stayin in the closet where it
belongs.

FROGGY: *(Almost in hysterics)* Fuckin waste of some
good heroin!

BAYLIS: It ain't a waste of shit! It's a reminder of were I
was nine months ago. Nine fuckin very scary months
ago. Besides, what do you know about west coast
heroin? On top of which, you've never spiked the shit
and you ain't about to. Not in front of me, anyway.

FROGGY: Gimme a square.

(He holds up the pack of cigarettes, teasing her.)

FROGGY: Gimme a square, Dickless.

*(He plucks a cigarette, throws it in the trash, a la the
dictionary. She picks it out of the trash, crosses to him for
a light. He lights it, she smokes, continues pacing by the
window, peering out, starts doing Kung Fu moves, crosses
to the T V sits in front of it.)*

FROGGY: I wish the T V worked. Why don't the T V work?

BAYLIS: It's dead.

FROGGY: TV's don't croak.

BAYLIS: What do they do, hibernate?

FROGGY: Dogs croak. Babies croak.

BAYLIS: I killed it.

FROGGY: Killed it how.

BAYLIS: I kicked it in.

FROGGY: Murdered the T V. Real good, Baylis.

BAYLIS: There ain't shit to watch anyways. Buncha fat-headed haircuts blowin around.

FROGGY: They got them Christmas specials on right now. The one's with the clay. Or commercials. I could watch commercials. Shampoo and stuff. Salad dressing. *(She crosses to the futon.)*

BAYLIS: Where'd you go today?

FROGGY: When?

BAYLIS: Earlier. I woke up and you were gone.

FROGGY: I didn't go nowhere.

BAYLIS: Well, you weren't here, goddamnit... You were over at the Port Authority again, weren't you?

(She exhales a great cloud of smoke, scratches her arms.)

BAYLIS: I'm right, ain't it. You went to the bus station fiendin for a fix. You went lookin for Pinchback.

FROGGY: I didn't go to the buttfuckin bus station and I wasn't lookin for Pinchback. He prolly ain't even there no more.

BAYLIS: He's either at the Port Authority or he's at Ryker's gettin bent over a foosball desk.

FROGGY: I hope he is. Fuckin buttfucker.

BAYLIS: Stop clawin at yourself.

FROGGY: My arms itch.

BAYLIS: You're gonna draw blood. Knock it off!

(She crosses to the bed, leans back starts massaging her hip. BAYLIS *drinks.)*

BAYLIS: Where'd you go, Avenue fuckin C?

FROGGY: I went to the doctor.

BAYLIS: You went to the *doctor.*

FROGGY: To a clinic.

BAYLIS: Bullshit.

FROGGY: I ain't lyin.

BAYLIS: What the hell's wrong with your hip?

FROGGY: Nothin.

BAYLIS: You act like you're old.

FROGGY: It aches, okay?

BAYLIS: That's all that fuckin and suckin. Shit wears your bones thin.

(She rubs her hip sockets.)

BAYLIS: What the hell did you go to a clinic for— charity? Think they're gonna give you a shot of Demerol or some shit? A little pro bono narcotic for the sweet and needy?

FROGGY: I went for results, okay, Fuckface?

BAYLIS: Results what kinda results?

FROGGY: I ain't tellin you.

BAYLIS: Why not?

FROGGY: Cause you're a fucking fuckface dickless faggit who poops in his pants!

(The chair flies. BAYLIS starts violently toward FROGGY. She runs to the closet, closes the door. BAYLIS stops suddenly and reaches for his lower back, doubles over in pain.)

(The phone rings. BAYLIS thaws out of his clench, answers the phone.)

BAYLIS: Hello?... Yeah, that's me.... Uh-huh... Uh-huh... Sewin me, for what—bein ugly?

(FROGGY comes out of the closet holding an aluminum baseball bat.)

BAYLIS: He put his hands on me first, he was askin for it... Uh-huh... Well, good luck, cause I don't got it and if I did I wouldn't pay him anyway.... Maybe next time he'll think twice before touchin his fellow man. *(He slams the phone down, slowly re-sets the chair.)* Fuck!

FROGGY: Who was that?

BAYLIS: Some lawyer.

FROGGY: What did he want?

BAYLIS: Last month when me and Murl were at the Orange Bear, this rich Portuguese fucker was mouthin off about some goddamn thing. One thing led to another and he put his hands on me so I stove his head in. He's claimin he needs plastic surgery. Says he's suin me. Ha!

FROGGY: You think you're like Chuck Norris or somethin.

BAYLIS: Fucker. *(He smokes, drinks.)*

FROGGY: Baylis, I went to the clinic cause my piss was brown.

BAYLIS: Your piss was brown?

FROGGY: Uh-huh.

BAYLIS: Brown like blood?

FROGGY: Brown like a puddle. And I've been gettin pains in my side.

BAYLIS: What side?

FROGGY: Right side under my ribs.

BAYLIS: What kinda pains?

FROGGY: *(Rising, pacing)* Like someone's kickin me. And I'm always tired. Sometimes I'm walkin on Canal and I feel like just layin down and sleepin. Right on the street like a bum.

BAYLIS: Jesus Christ, why didn't you say somethin?

FROGGY: I don't know. I thought it would go away, I guess. I heard Murl talkin about a clinic when he was over last time.

BAYLIS: He was talkin about an abortion clinic, Froggy.

FROGGY: Well that's where I went and this nurse told me about this other place on the west side so I went over there and they did a bunch of tests sucked my blood out looked at it they got real clean needles over there Baylis I almost took some cause I wanted to try that Blackfoot I was—

BAYLIS: Stop!

(She stops.)

BAYLIS: Quit actin like a goddamn drug addict!... Put the bat back in the closet.

(She crosses to the closet, returns the bat, closes the closet door.)

BAYLIS: Froggy, why didn't you tell me about your piss?

FROGGY: I don't know.

BAYLIS: You think it's just gonna go away?

FROGGY: It don't matter.

BAYLIS: It does matter, Froggy. It's your fuckin piss.

FROGGY: You couldn'ta come anyways.

BAYLIS: I coulda tried.

FROGGY: You can't even walk more than a block
without poopin your pants. You ain't goin nowhere.

BAYLIS: But I woulda tried, Froggy, I woulda. *(He
drinks.)* Well, what the hell did they say at the clinic?

FROGGY: I got somethin.

BAYLIS: Like *something* somethin?

FROGGY: Uh-huh.

BAYLIS: What—V D?

FROGGY: Hepatitis.

BAYLIS: You got hepatitis?

FROGGY: Yep.

BAYLIS: You got fuckin *hepatitis?*

FROGGY: Uh-huh. My arms are yellow, see?

(She shows him the insides of her arms.)

BAYLIS: Do you even know what that is?

FROGGY: Somethin with my liver.

BAYLIS: You're damn right it's somethin with your liver.

FROGGY: Like it's bruised.

BAYLIS: It's inflammation of the liver. Inflammation of
the fuckin liver! Jesus Christmas, Froggy, how did that
happen?

FROGGY: I don't know.

BAYLIS: Well what the hell are you gonna do?

FROGGY: Take these pills they gave me. They said I got a fever, too.

BAYLIS: Of course you got a fever, it's an infection. How high is it?

FROGGY: A hundred and somethin.

BAYLIS: Come here.

(She crosses to him, sits in his lap. He feels her forehead, pushes her off his lap opens the cooler, takes out a beer, opens it, sets it at the corner of the desk.)

BAYLIS: You gotta drink liquids, Froggy. I got a high fever like that once and it damn near made my teeth fall out. Liquids.

(She crosses to the bed, opens her lunch box, which is full of candy wrappers and junk food.)

FROGGY: *(Shoving candy in her mouth)* This doctor tried to stick a thermometer up my butt cause I wouldn't let him put it in my mouth.

BAYLIS: Why wouldn't you let him put it in your mouth?

FROGGY: I don't know. Fuckin fuckface kept lookin at my teeth and talkin about my gums and stuff. He said they were weak. They made me poop in a pan, too. They said it was pale.

BAYLIS: Are you takin the pills?

FROGGY: Uh-huh. I took two so far.

BAYLIS: Let me see em.

(She roots through the lunch box, candy wrappers flying, finds a bottle of pills crosses to him, hands them to him, crosses back to her lunch box. He studies the label.)

BAYLIS: These are fuckin vitamins.

FROGGY: They said that's all they could gimme. B and C and stuff.

BAYLIS: They charge you for these?

FROGGY: Nu-uh. They said I could go back and get more next week. I told the doctor about bein with you and stuff and he said it would be a good idea for you to go get a shot of gum goblins.

BAYLIS: Gum goblins?

(She finds a piece of paper in her lunch boxm hands it to him. He opens it, reads.)

BAYLIS: Gamma globulin.

FROGGY: What's that?

BAYLIS: Fuck if I know. I ain't gettin it, though.

FROGGY: He said it would be a good idea.

BAYLIS: I hate clinics. Too many lines. Methadone man pushin Tang at you. Plastic cups every goddamn where.

FROGGY: They said I shouldn't screw. No screwing. But I can still suck dick as long as I don't swallow. The doctor said the vitamins might work if I rest and stuff.

BAYLIS: He said they *might* work?

FROGGY: He said you never really know with hepatitis. Especially cause I've prolly had it for a while without even knowin cause of how I'm turnin yellow. I couldn't understand him too good, though. I think he was German or French or somethin.

BAYLIS: And what if the vitamins don't work?

FROGGY: I don't know. I'll prolly croak.

BAYLIS: Do you even care?

FROGGY: Sure.

BAYLIS: Does your side hurt right now?

FROGGY: A little.

BAYLIS: I got aspirin, you want some aspirin?

FROGGY: I want some heroin.

BAYLIS: Yeah, I know you do.

FROGGY: Every time the doctor said somethin about my liver I kept seein meat at the butcher's. How they chop up the cow butts with cleavers and stuff. How they wrap it in newspaper and how some old lady takes it home and cooks it in a pan.

BAYLIS: What about your parents?

FROGGY: What about em?

BAYLIS: Maybe you should make a phone call. They might be able to help you. Put you in a goddamn hospital or somethin.

FROGGY: I don't like hospitals.

BAYLIS: They got good grub in the hospital.

FROGGY: Too many cops.

BAYLIS: You gotta tell your parents, Froggy.

FROGGY: Fuckem.

BAYLIS: They don't even know where you are, do they?

FROGGY: Neither do yours.

BAYLIS: My parents are dead.

FROGGY: That sucks. Can I get another square?

BAYLIS: You smoked my whole goddamn pack.

(He throws her another cigarette. She lights it, smokes.)

BAYLIS: Jesus fuckin Christmas. Hepatitis. That's like *cancer* and shit.... *I'll* call your parents for fucksake. *(He grabs the phone.)* What's your name, Froggy?

(She stares back at him.)

BAYLIS: Just your goddamn last name so I can call information.

FROGGY: Gimme the heroin.

(From his shirt pocket, BAYLIS *removes an Altoids box containing snortable heroin. She quickly rises and crosses to the desk.)*

FROGGY: It's so yellow.

(He closes the box.)

BAYLIS: Your name.

FROGGY: My name's Froggy.

BAYLIS: Come on, I'm serious.

FROGGY: Froggy the Frog. Ribbit, ribbit.

BAYLIS: *(Starting for the window)* I'll throw it out the fuckin window. Let the pigeons nod on it.

FROGGY: Dr and Mrs Chalmer Cunningham eleven-twenty-seven Rob Roy Court Bloomfield Hills Michigan four-eight-three-oh-four area code two four eight six four five three one three one.

(He sits back down, gives the box back to FROGGY *and grabs the phone.)*

BAYLIS: Just two bumps, Froggy. Two goddamn bumps and that's it.

(She snorts the heroin while he dials the number. He waits. He slams the phone down.)

BAYLIS: Fuckin long distance got cut off. Fuck.

(He takes the box back just as she's trying to cut another line. She crosses to the bed and starts to nod.)

BAYLIS: Gimme that number again.

*(*FROGGY *giggles.)*

BAYLIS: Come on, I'm serious now.

(She giggles.)

BAYLIS: The fuckin number, Froggy!

FROGGY: *(Singsong)* Two four eight six four five three
one three one.

*(He writes it down in the dictionary, dials the phone again.
During the phone call, FROGGY starts to throw candy at him.
She might also flirt with BAYLIS sexually, mock
masturbating, trying to distract him.)*

BAYLIS: Hey Murl, it's Baylis...Baylis...Fucking *Baylis*
you moron!... Look, I need you to do me a favor.
My long distance got cut off again... I know, I know
fuck me with a crowbar...This mornin...I need you to
call this number.... Yeah, it's long distance.... Michigan...
Come on, man it'll just take a second...
   Murl, put the Makers down and do an old friend a
favor, huh? It'll take you two goddamn seconds...
Well, *get* a pen you fatfuck...
   Okay, you ready? ...Two four eight six four five three
one three one. Call that number and ask the *Doctor* to
call me here...The *Doctor*... No, he's not a fuckin *dealer*,
Murl, he's legit...
   I don't even *know* the dude, Murl, how the fuck would
I score somethin?...
   It's for Froggy... Yeah, she's still here.... Yeah, she's
movin in and we're gettin married. We're on our way
to the courthouse right now... Yeah, I'm wearin a
goddamn tux. It's fire engine red... No, you dumbshit,
I'm kidding....
   Yeah, fuck you too, Murl... Just make that call, okay?
Tell him it's about his daughter... The *Doctor*... Okay,
cool. I owe you one....
   No, I haven't tried it yet. It numbs you, right?...
(He removes a small vial of Novocain, stares at it.) I know,
I know, you said it a hundred times. 'Novocain,
Novocain, shoot the muscle, not the vein.' Yeah,
I could use some numbin... All right. Later.

(He hangs up, puts the vial back in his pocket, drinks from the whiskey bottle. FROGGY *is wearing her hat again, and is starting to put her shirts back on.)*

BAYLIS: What are you doin?

FROGGY: Dressin.

BAYLIS: You ain't leavin are you?

FROGGY: They told me to keep warm.

BAYLIS: Jesus Christ, then why'd you take your damn clothes off in the first place?

FROGGY: Cause you told me to.

BAYLIS: You know, Froggy, sometimes you pretend you're stupid and you know damn well you ain't stupid.

FROGGY: I never said I was stupid.

BAYLIS: I actually think you're pretty goddamn smart, how do you like that.

FROGGY: I don't wanna be smart. Smart people don't know shit.

BAYLIS: See what I mean, that's smart. What you just said is smart as hell.

FROGGY: Can I get another square?

BAYLIS: Negative.

FROGGY: *(Mocking)* Negative.

BAYLIS: I ain't goin to bed with an empty pack again.

*(*FROGGY *crosses to the desk.)*

FROGGY: How's your thing?

BAYLIS: It's fuckin murderin me's how it is.

FROGGY: What happened to those pain killers?

BAYLIS: You *took* half the fuckers is what happened to em.

FROGGY: Nu-uh.

BAYLIS: Froggy, last night I saw you crushin up my codeine and tryin to snort it. Yeah, you thought I was sleepin. Goddamn larceny.

FROGGY: So get more.

BAYLIS: Doctor won't write me another prescription. He thinks I'm hooked. Old ethical bastard. Froggy the goddamn larcenist.

(He gives her a cigarette. She hides it in her hat. She gently places her foot in his crotch.)

FROGGY: Do some heroin.

BAYLIS: Not likely.

FROGGY: Why not.

BAYLIS: Cause I'm savin it for you, you fiend.

FROGGY: You want me to suck your dick? I could suck your dick.

BAYLIS: No, I don't want you to suck my dick.

FROGGY: What about Murl's?

BAYLIS: Why the hell would you suck Murl's dick?

FROGGY: I don't know. I thought maybe you owed him some money or somethin.

BAYLIS: You stay away from that fat sonuvabitch. I don't ever want you doin that for him again, you hear? That was before.

FROGGY: Before what?

BAYLIS: Before I really knew you before. Before you left Pinchback before. Before you stopped dancin before. Before when I owed Murl money before. I don't owe him shit no more and I don't plan on it. And besides, that fat motherfucker blew his load in your mouth.

FROGGY: So.

BAYLIS: Listen to you, so.

FROGGY: It's like puddin. I don't care.

BAYLIS: Yeah, you don't care about shit do you?

FROGGY: You want me to go down to Mr Templeton's and suck his dick for the rent again?

BAYLIS: I want you to stay right here. Right here in that bed.

(He shoos her off the desk. She crosses back to the bed lays down.)

BAYLIS: You ain't goin nowhere. And you ain't suckin nobody's dick. Jesus Christ, Froggy, sometimes I think you'd suck off a German Shepherd if it asked you to.

FROGGY: Why don't you want me to suck yours?

BAYLIS: Cause.

FROGGY: Cause why?

BAYLIS: Just cause, now drop it.

FROGGY: It's okay if you can't get it up no more, I still like doin it.

BAYLIS: Stop talkin like that, Froggy.

FROGGY: It's prolly cause you drink all that Jack.

BAYLIS: It's cause of my back and you know it's cause of my back. The nerve is inflamed and it's fuckin with my prostrate. I don't need any goddamn lectures from you.

FROGGY: I'll pinch your nipples.

BAYLIS: No.

FROGGY: I'll pinch em till they're purple.

BAYLIS: Knock it off!

FROGGY: Tuck me in.

(BAYLIS *wheels over to the bed, tucks her in.*)

FROGGY: Hey, Baylis.

BAYLIS: What.

FROGGY: Did you mean what you said before?

BAYLIS: Before when?

FROGGY: When you were talkin to Murl.

BAYLIS: What did I say?

FROGGY: About marryin me.

BAYLIS: I was jokin.

FROGGY: I'd marry you, Baylis. I'd marry you cause you're good at tellin me what to do. I like it.

BAYLIS: Why don't you just go ahead and nod off. Have a good nod now.

FROGGY: My dad used to tell me what to do. He was good at it, too. I'd start to do stuff and he'd tell me to stop.

(BAYLIS *gets in his chair, wheels over to the desk.*)

FROGGY: If I was gonna croak would you marry me?

BAYLIS: You ain't gonna croak.

FROGGY: But if I was?

BAYLIS: I don't know.

FROGGY: You can say no, I don't care.

BAYLIS: I wouldn't be much of a husband.

FROGGY: That's okay. We'd be together. Froggy and Baylis.

BAYLIS: We're together now.

FROGGY: Okay.

(The sound of footsteps in the hallway. They freeze, look at each other.)

FROGGY: Templeton?—

BAYLIS: Sshshshs!

(The footsteps continue. BAYLIS crosses to the closet, grabs the baseball bat. He approaches the door listens. The footsteps fade. The phone rings. BAYLIS puts the baseball bat back in the closet, crosses to the phone, answers it.)

BAYLIS: Hello?... Murl? Hey, man, you make that call?... Yeah, what'd he say?... Uh-huh... Uh-huh... Uh-huh... Okay... Thanks, buddy...
   No, I ain't sendin her over... She ain't doin that no more, Murl. No way... I don't give a shit! Besides you were on the phone for what—two whole fuckin minutes?
   ...Okay... Okay...
   Merry Christmas to you, too, you crooked sonuvabitch. Eat a fuckin turkey. Later. *(He hangs up the phone.)*

BAYLIS: How you feelin?

FROGGY: Okay.

BAYLIS: You want me to go get you some grub? Mickey Dees or somethin?

FROGGY: I'd puke.

BAYLIS: You're sweatin pretty bad, Froggy.

FROGGY: I like it. Feels like I'm disappearing.

(He wheels over to her with the beer, sets it near her head.)

BAYLIS: Drink that, it'll cool you down.

(She drinks. She vomits on the floor.)

FROGGY: Sorry.

BAYLIS: It's okay, Froggy. It's okay. I'll clean it.
(He crosses to her with a roll of toilet paper.)

FROGGY: My dad said I croaked, didn't he.

(He cleans the puke.)

FROGGY: Didn't he.

(BAYLIS doesn't respond, finishes cleaning.)

FROGGY: He prolly said I croaked three years ago.

(BAYLIS stares at her a moment.)

FROGGY: It's okay. I don't care.

(BAYLIS starts for the garbage. Suddenly there is a pecking sound at the window pane. BAYLIS lurches toward the window as if he is about to attack a man, army style.)

BAYLIS: Hey! *(He slaps at the window several times.)*
Get, you!... Goddamn thing's drivin me crazy.

FROGGY: You're like Chuck Norris and stuff.

BAYLIS: I don't like the fucker.

FROGGY: How can you not like a bird?

BAYLIS: I just don't. It's greedy!

FROGGY: I saw its tongue today. It looked like a worm.
Like a little blue worm.

BAYLIS: What the hell is a blackbird doin on Canal
Street anyways? *(He grabs a roll of electric tape hanging from a nail on the wall, tears off a strip, covers the old piece on the window.)*

FROGGY: It was just sittin on the other side of the
window. Starin all funny like it knew me. I could
see its eye. It looked plastic. Like it was from a doll.

(He crosses back to the desk.)

BAYLIS: Goddamn thing keeps peckin at the crack like it wants in. Why can't it go fuck a pigeon or somethin? Leave us alone.

FROGGY: I like it. It acts like it knows me.

BAYLIS: If I had a gun I'd shoot the fucker. Goddamn blackbird... (*He sits.*)

FROGGY: It hurts to swallow.

BAYLIS: I'll hit the deli. Get you some water.

FROGGY: Hey, Baylis.

BAYLIS: Hey, what.

FROGGY: What'd you do before you hurt your thing?

BAYLIS: It's called a disc.

FROGGY: What'd you do before you hurt your dick? Just kidding.

BAYLIS: I worked for a movin company. I already told you that.

FROGGY: I know, but before that.

BAYLIS: I was in the service.

FROGGY: How long.

BAYLIS: Three years.

FROGGY: You were a soldier?

BAYLIS: Yep.

FROGGY: Where?

BAYLIS: Bootcamped at Fort Knox, Kentucky. Stationed at Fort Stewart, Georgia.

FROGGY: Like on the commercial. Be all you can be and stuff?

BAYLIS: Yeah, be all you can fuckin be.

FROGGY: What were you, like a janitor?

BAYLIS: I was an E-3.

FROGGY: You were a letter?

BAYLIS: E-3's a private first class. P F C.

FROGGY: I used to want to be a letter. Like on Sesame Street with Grover and stuff. I wanted to grow up to be the letter M.

BAYLIS: P F C ain't shit. It's like bein a waiter.

FROGGY: Get it any fights?

BAYLIS: Some.

FROGGY: Murl says you're a good fighter.

BAYLIS: He does, does he?

FROGGY: Yeah, but I think you punch like a pussy.

BAYLIS: I don't punch you, Froggy. I just bat you around a little. Keep you in line.

FROGGY: I know. I like it.

(BAYLIS *drinks*.)

BAYLIS: All types of lowlifes in the Army. Buncha scoundrels and halfwits out there defendin our freedom.

FROGGY: Did you go anywhere fancy?

BAYLIS: Not really. Only left the country once. Did a tour in Saudi Arabia during Desert Storm.

FROGGY: What's that?

BAYLIS: You never heard of *Desert Storm*?

FROGGY: Sounds like a video game. Like PlayStation or somethin.

BAYLIS: It was a *war*. In the Middle East. The Gulf War.

FROGGY: My dad used to go golfing. He wore these clothes that looked like ice cream. Pink shirts and stuff.

BAYLIS: *Gulf.* G-U-L-F. Gulf as in bay. Not fucking *golf.*

FROGGY: You should have like a fake leg and an eye patch and stuff.

BAYLIS: Very funny.

FROGGY: There was this old Vet who used to watch me dance. He had a plastic eye. Used to pop it out and float it in his beer. Then he'd wink at me. You could see the meat in his head. He was like sixty.

BAYLIS: He was prolly in Nam.

FROGGY: You kill anyone?

BAYLIS: I don't know.

FROGGY: How come you don't know?

BAYLIS: Cause it was dark.

FROGGY: Sounds like bein at a club. Did they give you a gun?

BAYLIS: It's called a weapon. M-16.

FROGGY: Was it heavy?

BAYLIS: Not really. Like carryin an electric guitar.

FROGGY: I used to dream about guns.

(BAYLIS *shoots her a look.*)

FROGGY: I mean weapons. Big silver cowboy pistols. Like the fake ones at Toys R Us. But in my dreams they were real. I'd shoot cars. Cars and churches. I shot Jesus once, too. He was up on the cross lookin all sad and stuff. Shot him right in the balls... Did any of your friends croak?

BAYLIS: Nope. Saw some go crazy, though. There was this big black kid from Houston—Watty. On paper he was the baddest motherfucker in boots. Six-five, two-fifty. Blacker than coal, this kid. Blueblack, they called him. In the barracks, nobody would fuck with him, not even the N C Os.

So we're in formation. First Sergeant's takin reports and there's some gunfire in the distance. Wasn't nowhere near us. All the sudden, Watty goes to a knee. I'm standin next to him. I look over and he's clutchin his chest like he got shot or some shit. Turns out the motherfucker got so scared he had a heart attack. Twenty-three, twenty-four years old. A fuckin heart attack, big strong guy like that.

FROGGY: Did he croak?

BAYLIS: Nope. After he recovered they sent his ass home. Back to his mama in Houston. I guess it's that fight or flight thing. Are you a lion or a lamb? Big strong guy like that.

FROGGY: Did you get shot or anything?

BAYLIS: Nope. All in all, the war was okay. Learned how to play hearts and ate a lot of chicken cacciatore.

FROGGY: So you're like a veterinarian and stuff.

BAYLIS: *Veteran.* Unless you get hurt and win a medal, the only nice thing about bein a Vet is when you die you get a free Military burial. Arlington, Virginia. They put a little flag on your headstone and everything.

FROGGY: When I croak I don't wanna be buried.

BAYLIS: What, you wanna be cremated?

FROGGY: I just want someone to roll me in a blanket and put me in a dumpster.

BAYLIS: At least it would be cheap.

FROGGY: Once you're croaked you're croaked, that's the way I see it.

BAYLIS: Hell, I'll take the military burial. Fuck it,
why not? At least there's a place where someone
can come visit you. Piss on your grave or somethin.

FROGGY: They'd prolly poop on your grave.

BAYLIS: Hey.

(She makes a farting noise. He checks the bandage on his foot.)

FROGGY: What'd you do after that desert thing?

BAYLIS: Why you so interested in this stuff all the
sudden?

FROGGY: I don't know. It's like goin to the movies or
somethin.

BAYLIS: Hollywood fuckin story, right?

FROGGY: Come on, Baylis, tell me what happened after
Desert Thunder.

BAYLIS: Desert *Storm.*

FROGGY: Go on.

(He starts to get dressed.)

BAYLIS: I came back. Moved to Chicago. Got married.
Tried to go to school on the G I bill. Dropped out after
a semester cause I couldn't stand sittin in a classroom.
Moved to San Francisco for a while. Bought a guitar.
Tried to write music. Came to New York. Found that
basic-ass typewriter over there on the sidewalk. Tried
to write stories and shit.

FROGGY: Why'd you stop?

BAYLIS: Wasn't good. At any of it.

FROGGY: What happened to the guitar?

BAYLIS: Lost it in that game of hearts that Murl used to
run on Thursdays.

FROGGY: Were you like unplugged and stuff?

BAYLIS: It was an acoustic, yes. Second-hand Fender. Pretty little blond thing. Jumped out of tune a lot but I liked it.

FROGGY: You were prolly like Mr Groove Control and stuff. Mr Groovalicious Groovecontrol.

BAYLIS: Well, Murl's got it now. Keeps it in his closet. Shot the Moon on my ass. Me, Footy and Kent. Bastard don't even use it.

FROGGY: You got a nice voice.

BAYLIS: How do you know?

FROGGY: I can just tell. The way you talk and stuff.

(BAYLIS *puts his boots on.*)

FROGGY: I wish you had it now.

BAYLIS: I woulda prolly wound up smashin the damn thing against the wall anyways.

FROGGY: Now I'm like your guitar.

BAYLIS: Yeah you are, ain't you. Noisy.

FROGGY: You can play me to sleep.

(BAYLIS *gathers his keys off the desk.*)

FROGGY: Hey, Baylis.

BAYLIS: *(Sitting)* What.

FROGGY: If you didn't see me dancin at Harmony where do you think we'd be right now?

BAYLIS: I don't know.

FROGGY: Make somethin up.

BAYLIS: Let's see. I imagine *I'd* be right here in this room flattening my own ass and you'd be over there strippin for the fatfucks at Harmony.

FROGGY: Maybe you'd be a cop and I'd be a bus driver?

BAYLIS: Doubt it.

FROGGY: You'd arrest me for gettin high on the bus and stuff.

BAYLIS: I'd more than arrest you.

FROGGY: Tell me what it was like to watch me.

BAYLIS: It was fuckin beatific.

FROGGY: Tell me, Dickless.

BAYLIS: You were up there under the lights. Dancin to Chaka Kahn or some goddamn thing.

FROGGY: Prince!

BAYLIS: Yeah, *Prince*. What a genius. I was standin in the back, waitin for Murl to come up from downstairs. He was scorin some X off that guy who runs the place. Juco.

FROGGY: Jelco.

BAYLIS: Yeah, Jelco—that Serbian guy. Anyway, you came slinkin down that stage thing—

FROGGY: The runway.

BAYLIS: The runaway.

FROGGY: *Run*way.

BAYLIS: Runway runaway - whatever. You came slinkin down the thing like some kind of goddamn cat you see in a zoo. Leanin real nice. Makin eyes with every bastard in the front row. The Wall Street suits. The college kids. Other women. I couldn't take my eyes off you. Nobody in the room could take their eyes off you. You musta collected a cold hundred in singles. Then the music changed and you disappeared and some fat chick in a wet suit walked on stage and it was like somethin beautiful had died. Like when a tree falls apart or somethin.

FROGGY: Keep goin.

BAYLIS: When you came out you were dressed in all your goddamn thermals. Sweatpants. Tennis shoes. That crazy hat you like to wear. I thought you were some kid from the little league who snuck through the window in the men's bathroom. No one recognized you, but I did. I recognized the hell right out of you. Kept askin you your name but all you would say was "Froggy", "Froggy".

FROGGY: And you didn't have no girlfriend.

BAYLIS: No, I definitely didn't have a girlfriend.

FROGGY: Cause you were married.

BAYLIS: I'd just gotten divorced.

FROGGY: And your wife left you cause you wouldn't eat her pussy.

BAYLIS: That's not true, Froggy.

FROGGY: Yes it is.

BAYLIS: She left me cause I couldn't make a fuckin baby with her, that's why she left me.

FROGGY: That's not what you told me.

BAYLIS: Well, that's the reason. (*He drinks.*)

FROGGY: Do you miss her?

BAYLIS: No.

FROGGY: Me neither.

BAYLIS: How the hell could you miss her, she was my wife.

FROGGY: I don't miss people.

BAYLIS: What do you miss, stop signs?

FROGGY: I miss rain and stuff like that. Fog.

BAYLIS: You're too damn stubborn to miss anybody. *(He drinks.)*

FROGGY: Where is she?

BAYLIS: Who, my wife?

FROGGY: Your wife-alicous.

BAYLIS: I don't know. She was in Chicago, last I heard.

FROGGY: What's her name?

BAYLIS: Peg.

FROGGY: Pegalicous.

BAYLIS: Peggy Peg.

FROGGY: Do you still love her?

BAYLIS: No.

FROGGY: When you could still get it up did you used to fantasize about her?

BAYLIS: I used to fantasize about you.

FROGGY: How could you fantasize about me, you were with me.

BAYLIS: I don't know. When we were fuckin I guess I used to pretend like we were together in some real way. Like we were livin in a house and I had a job with benefits. Pension plan. A couple of beagles. Stupid shit like that. *(He starts to gather the things for his pockets.)*

FROGGY: Can I have some more heroin?

BAYLIS: Negative.

FROGGY: Okay.

BAYLIS: You should try and get some sleep. I'm gonna go get you that water.

(BAYLIS *crosses to the futon.* FROGGY *grabs the handcuffs that are attached to the bike chains, hands them to* BAYLIS. *He cuffs her.)*

FROGGY: I'd make a baby with you, Baylis.

BAYLIS: No you wouldn't.

FROGGY: Yes I would. We could raise it right here.

BAYLIS: Froggy, you couldn't make a fuckin baby with me cause I'm the one who can't make a baby. I'm sterile.

FROGGY: Oh.

BAYLIS: See? You're tryin to act stupid again and you ain't stupid.

FROGGY: Hey, Baylis.

BAYLIS: Hey, Froggy.

FROGGY: Can I maybe shoot some of that Novocain stuff?

BAYLIS: Denied.

FROGGY: Okay... Hey, Baylis.

BAYLIS: Hey, Froggy.

FROGGY: Will you do me a favor?

BAYLIS: What.

FROGGY: Sing me a song.

BAYLIS: Negative.

FROGGY: Please? I'll give you my arm and you can pretend it's your guitar. It'll be fun.

BAYLIS: Not a chance.

FROGGY: Pretty please with heroin on top? I'll stop beggin for squares and stuff. Just one song.

(BAYLIS *watches her for a moment.)*

BAYLIS: All right. One song. But I ain't singin the whole thing.

FROGGY: Why not?

BAYLIS: Cause my memory sucks shit.

FROGGY: Okay.

BAYLIS: And don't make fun of me or I won't do it again.

FROGGY: I won't.

BAYLIS: And stop callin me Dickless. You can call me Fuckface, but don't call me Dickless.

FROGGY: Okay, Dickless. Just kidding.

(BAYLIS *crosses to the bed, sits. She offers her arm. He holds it, tunes it as a guitar for a moment, starts to sing. The song is light and fun and should lose momentum toward the end.)*

BAYLIS: *(Singing)*
it's easy to sit on a stool
it's easy to find your way down
it's easy to fish
it's easy to wish
it's easy to laugh at a clown

take care of the things that you find
take care of the Bethlehem tree
take care of my boat
take care of my goat
take care of my dog
take care of her please

it's only a few days away
it's only a few moments more
it's only the night
it's only the night
it's only a face at my door

remember the size of my hands
remember the length of my bones

remember my skin
remember my sins
remember my breath...

(BAYLIS *trails off, releases her arm.*)

FROGGY: That was nice.

(No response)

FROGGY: That was so groovalicious, Baylis. It was like a song. When'd you write that?

BAYLIS: When I lived in Chicago. It's better with the guitar.

FROGGY: What's it called?

BAYLIS: Never named it.

FROGGY: What's it about?

BAYLIS: I don't know. Nothin.

FROGGY: You should name it.

BAYLIS: I don't like namin songs.

FROGGY: You could call it the Froggy Song.

(He laughs.)

FROGGY: I like the part about the goat and the boat.

BAYLIS: The goatboat.

FROGGY: And when you go it's easy to fish it's easy to wish.

BAYLIS: Fishwish. A two-cent rhyme.

FROGGY: You could be like it's easy to *poop*, too. *(Singing)* It's easy to poop, it's easy to poop.... Just kidding.

BAYLIS: Damn song's too monotonous.

FROGGY: No it ain't.

(BAYLIS *looks to the whiskey bottle, but realizes he's on the bed.*)

FROGGY: Hey, Baylis.

BAYLIS: Hey, Froggy.

FROGGY: Will you keep holdin my arm?

(*She offers her arm again. He holds it. They are quiet for a moment.*)

FROGGY: Hey, Baylis.

BAYLIS: Hey, Froggy.

FROGGY: You know that code I was tappin before?

BAYLIS: Uh-huh.

FROGGY: It was special. One four three.

BAYLIS: One four three. What's that, one of them dealer codes?

FROGGY: Nu-uh. It's my code. But I ain't gonna tell you what it is.

BAYLIS: Suit yourself.

FROGGY: My other arm feels like it's missin.

(*He rubs her arms for a moment.*)

FROGGY: Rubalicious.

(*He stops rubbing. She's fighting to stay awake.*)

FROGGY: Hey, Baylis.

BAYLIS: Hey, Froggy

FROGGY: Do me a favor?

BAYLIS: What.

FROGGY: Get me some crayons. I feel like coloring.

BAYLIS: I'll get you some crayons.

FROGGY: And don't leave till I fall asleep.

BAYLIS: Okay.

FROGGY: Promise?

BAYLIS: I won't leave. I'll stay right here.

FROGGY: And tell me to go to sleep again.

BAYLIS: Go to sleep again.

FROGGY: Come on, say it for real.

BAYLIS: Go to sleep.

FROGGY: Okay. Again?

BAYLIS: Go to sleep, Froggy.

(BAYLIS *stays with* FROGGY *until she falls asleep. After that he crosses to the window and looks out. He touches the crack and checks the electric tape. He then crosses to the desk, grabs his bottle of whiskey, drinks while crossing to the door, limping. When he reaches the door he sets the bottle down, puts his leather jacket on, turns the light off, exits. When the door closes,* FROGGY *gets out of bed, crosses to the closet, tries to stretch her chains so she can reach the closet door, fails, tries again, fails. The sound of pecking at the window.* FROGGY *turns to the window, stands very still, waves to something. She waves with very small gestures, childlike. Then she makes a few very simple flapping motions with her arms, nothing big, very tiny. After this she crosses back to bed, lies down, sleeps. Low's* Above and Below *plays as the lights fade to black.)*

END OF ACT ONE

ACT TWO

(Later)

(Low's Bright *plays as lights fade up.)*

(FROGGY is asleep in the bed. She is bundled up, wearing her hat.)

(BAYLIS enters. He is limping awkwardly, in excruciating pain, moving very slowly. Dried blood trails from his forehead down the side of his neck. He bends down to pick up the whiskey that he had left by the door, drinks desperately, rises, crosses to FROGGY. He is holding a bottle of drinking water and a brown grocery bag. He sets the water on the floor, feels her forehead, unlocks her handcuffs, then crosses to the desk, sets the grocery bag on the desk, removes his coat, his shoes, crosses to the closet.)

(FROGGY wakes and watches him.)

(BAYLIS takes his pants down. He is wearing a pair of adult diapers. He has shit himself. He removes a container of Babywipes from the closet and attempts to clean up. When he is through, he steps into a fresh diaper, balls the soiled diaper into the towel, crosses to the brown paper bag, removes a loaf of bread, a few cans of soup, a pack of cigarettes, and a small carton of milk, a box of crayons. He unloads the items on the desk, stuffs the soiled diaper into the bag, makes a move to toss it in the garbage, smells the mess in his hands, then crosses to the door, opens it, and throws the bag in the hall, closes the door.)

*(He crosses back to the desk, slips into a pair of old
sweatpants, then kneels at the cooler, fills a spare plastic
bag with ice, sets the bag on his head.)*

*(There is a pecking at the window. Despite his pain,
BAYLIS rushes the window, starts slapping at it,
out of control. He stops suddenly.)*

BAYLIS: Fuck me.

(He checks his hand, turns, sees FROGGY watching him.)

BAYLIS: Hey.

FROGGY: Hey.

BAYLIS: Goddamn bird again. *(He grabs the electric tape,
attempts to repair the window.)*

FROGGY: What happened?

BAYLIS: I just broke the window.

FROGGY: I mean what happened to your head.

BAYLIS: Oh, I just got the shit kicked outta me.

FROGGY: By who?

BAYLIS: Some fuckin pussy cop.

FROGGY: What'd you do?

BAYLIS: Nothin! I'm comin up outta the subway and
this flatfoot starts hasslin me for no fuckin reason!
Askin where I'd been, where I'm goin, all that cause
I'm walkin funny! Thinks I'm drunk cause I got a limp!
I Ds me!
   I'm standin there with a loada shit in my pants
wonderin when I'm gonna be able to sit down and
end the pain and some brown-nosin rookie pig decides
it's time to spread a little Christmas cheer! Practically
knocks my goddamn head off! Right on the fuckin
stairs to the N-R! Writes me a two hundred dollar ticket
for public drunkenness or disorderly conduct or some

shit!
  Some public official! I'm the one who took that sand
nigger germ gas! Shootin blanks! My dick's about as
useful as a busted cap gun. *(to the window)* YEAH,
MEET ME IN IRAQ YOU FUCKIN NO-NECK PIG!!!
Motherfucker!

FROGGY: You okay?

BAYLIS: *(Crossing to desk)* Yeah, I'm fuckin happy as a
snowman. My back, my foot, now my goddamn head.

(He tosses her the crayons. She knocks twice on the floor.)

BAYLIS: You're welcome.

*(She empties the crayons on the bed, removes one of the
scraps of paper from under the futon mattress and starts
to draw.)*

FROGGY: What were you doin on the subway?

BAYLIS: I went over to Port Authority.

FROGGY: Score anything?

BAYLIS: Yeah, but not what you think.

FROGGY: You didn't get no heroin?

BAYLIS: No, I didn't get any more fuckin heroin, Froggy.
The weaning is over. I think you need to be about
through with that shit.

FROGGY: What'dja score?

BAYLIS: A bus ticket.

FROGGY: Where you goin?

BAYLIS: It ain't where I'm goin.

FROGGY: I ain't goin nowhere.

BAYLIS: Yes you are.

(She grabs her lunchbox, uses the back of it to draw on.)

BAYLIS: How you feelin?

FROGGY: I don't know.

BAYLIS: Better, worse, same?

FROGGY: Same I think.

BAYLIS: You sleep any?

FROGGY: Uh-huh.

BAYLIS: Got you that water. Soup and bread, too.
Carton of milk... Shit my fuckin pants again.

FROGGY: I know. I can smell it. Monkeys at the zoo.

BAYLIS: Already burned through another box of diapers.

FROGGY: It's cool how you just throw em away and
stuff. Like a paper plate with ketchup on it.

BAYLIS: I'm tired of livin like a goddamn toddler.
*(He tears off the back of the dictionary, attempts to patch
the broken glass.)*

FROGGY: You were gone forever.

BAYLIS: I had to try and convince Hammy the
Hamsandwich to cash my disability check.

FROGGY: Did he?

BAYLIS: No, little ruthless fucker. Too busy countin his
goddamn profit papers.

FROGGY: How'd you cash it?

BAYLIS: I went to Murl's and wrote it over to him.
Fuckin check cashin place is all boarded up. Giuliani's
too busy fillin potholes and polishin the billboards
in Times Square to keep the check cashin places open.
Can't even live in this city no more unless you got a
goddamn A T M card.
    Can't afford to pay Templeton half the time cause
they tax my disability so hard. It's goddamn extortion.

Livin on soup and grilled cheese sandwiches like
breakfast and dinner don't even exist.
   Then there's that goddamn blackbird always peckin
at the crack in the window. Templeton was sposed
to change the glass three months ago. Sideways
sonuvabitch. I told him to leave the stuff up here
and I'd fix the motherfucker!
(Crossing back to the chair) Chargin me three hundred a
month for a shoebox. Three hundred goddamn bucks
and not a drop of plumbing. He can't even keep the
cold out. *(to the door)* I SHOULD GO DOWN THERE
AND KICK HIM RIGHT IN HIS OVERSIZED ASS!
*(He crosses to front door, grabs whiskey, takes a nip,
crosses back to desk. Stopping)* You take your vitamins?

FROGGY: Throat hurts too much.

BAYLIS: Well, take em.

(She takes her vitamins, drinks from the jug.)

BAYLIS: You hungry?

FROGGY: No.

BAYLIS: Cigarette?

FROGGY: Nu-uh.

BAYLIS: Froggy the Frog turns down a cigarette?
It's a fuckin miracle.

FROGGY: Last one tasted funny. Like pennies in my
mouth.

BAYLIS: Your arms still itchin?

(She nods, shows him her arms. Red streaks)

BAYLIS: I was gonna get you some cortisone for that,
but then we wouldn'ta been able to eat. Askin Hammy
for a favor any more's like lookin for meat in a box of
fishsticks.

FROGGY: Where am I goin, Baylis?

BAYLIS: Detroit.

(They share a look.)

BAYLIS: It's for your own good, Froggy. Bus leaves tomorrow mornin, ten a.m.

(She starts to whistle.)

BAYLIS: Yeah, whistle till your lips turn blue, you're gettin on that bus.

FROGGY: What's it like outside?

BAYLIS: Colder than hell. Temperature's droppin so fast it's like someone's controllin it.

FROGGY: Is Canal all lit up and stuff?

BAYLIS: So many goddamn lights you can't even tell what's Christmas and what's traffic.

FROGGY: Is it snowin?

BAYLIS: Wish it was. It would make things look better, at least. So much goddamn dogshit on the sidewalk you'd think we lived in the third world. Fuckin Nicaragua.

FROGGY: You go by Harmony.

BAYLIS: Why would I go by Harmony?

FROGGY: I don't know. Look at some tits or somethin.

BAYLIS: I'm tired of lookin at tits. After a while they start lookin back at you. *(He dumps the ice back in the cooler, starts to cook a can of soup over a pack of Sterno.)* I had a hard enough time gettin to the goddamn deli, let alone to Port Authority. This sciatica shit's turnin me old and quick. I don't even feel like *eatin* half the time. Can't walk more than a block without havin to go to a knee.

   It woulda been one thing if I'da fucked up my back in Iraq. At least I woulda got a medal. Somethin to hock for the rent. But of course, I herniate my damn disc moving some rich fucker's *Tiffany sofa*. Some Park Avenue country club boy in a landowner's suit. And all I got to show for it's a chronic case of incontinence and fuckin mean streak wider than the goddamn Potomac.

FROGGY: Fotomat's ain't wide

BAYLIS: Potomac. It's a river.

FROGGY: What's incontinence?

BAYLIS: When you lose control of your bowels.

FROGGY: I'm innercontinent, too, Baylis.

BAYLIS: *In*continent. Trust me, you ain't incontinent, Froggy.

FROGGY: I pee my pants all the time.

BAYLIS: You piss your pants cause once you start noddin you're too satisfied to get up and go to the bathroom. That's called bein lazy.

FROGGY: I pee my pants cause I like it when you clean me.

BAYLIS: It's a real fuckin pleasure, let me tell you.

(FROGGY giggles.)

BAYLIS: Froggy, did you piss the bed again, goddamnit?

(FROGGY giggles.)

BAYLIS: Jesus Christmas, between the two of us, we've soiled more sheets than an old folks' home. Thank god for K-Mart. We'd be sleepin on fuckin newspapers. *(He crosses to the closet, gets a clean set of sheets and a towel, crosses to bed.)* You're gonna have to get up a minute.

(She offers her arms.)

BAYLIS: I can't lift you, Froggy.

*(She gets up, the blanket wrapped around her shoulders.
She crosses to the closet, grabs the Babywipes, and an old
pair of sweatpants, stands near his chair. On all fours
he removes the soiled sheet and attempts to tidy the bed.
She gets in his chair, starts twirling around, whistles at him.)*

BAYLIS: Stop starin at my butt.

FROGGY: You look like you got mush in your pants.

BAYLIS: Just what I need to hear. Great for the fuckin
confidence.

FROGGY: You got a nice butt, Baylis.

BAYLIS: Nice and goddamn itchy.

FROGGY: You should use lotions and stuff. Baby cream.

BAYLIS: I'm thirty-two years old and I got a goddamn
rash on my ass.

FROGGY: I'll wear the diapers with you.

(He snaps at her. She gets out of his chair.)

*(BAYLIS balls up the soiled sheet and towel, throws them
toward the closet, crawls to FROGGY at the desk. She opens
the blanket, revealing the Babywipes, happy to be cleaned.
He lowers her pants and underwear, cleans her. She flirts a
bit. He helps her into the sweatpants. There is some playful
physical stuff that turns to tenderness. FROGGY breaks away.)*

FROGGY: I wanna dance.

*(She crosses to her golf bag, removes a small cassette player,
gives it to BAYLIS, then returns to the futon, covers herself
with the blanket for a moment.)*

FROGGY: Don't start it yet. *(She stands facing the wall, her
limbs spread, still completely covered by the blanket.)* Okay.

*(BAYLIS engages the cassette player. Prince's Kiss plays.
At the end of the first guitar riff, Froggy turns and drops the
blanket. She is now wearing a purple wig that she had pulled*

from the golf bag. FROGGY *starts dancing. She is an amazing dancer, incredibly sexual. She flirts with* BAYLIS. *The dance evolves into something really fun for a moment, and then* FROGGY *suddenly falls.* BAYLIS *turns the cassette player off.)*

BAYLIS: You okay?

FROGGY: My legs gave out.

BAYLIS: Can you get up?

FROGGY: I think so.

BAYLIS: You need me to help you?

FROGGY: Maybe.

(He wheels over to her in the chair, helps her to her feet and back to the bed. She pulls the wig off, gets under the covers.)

FROGGY: Hey Baylis, that lawyer called again.

BAYLIS: Great. When?

FROGGY: Right after you left.

BAYLIS: What'd he want?

FROGGY: He said he just wanted to talk to you.

BAYLIS: Fuckin shark's prolly tryin to get me to settle out of court cause he knows I'll win.

FROGGY: So call him.

BAYLIS: Fuck him. I hate lawyers. I ain't payin that Portuguese bastard nothin.

FROGGY: The lawyer said he's gotta get plastic surgery and stuff.

BAYLIS: Oh, that's bullshit. I hit him in the forehead. How the hell can you get plastic surgery on your fuckin forehead? Jesus Christ, it's *Christmas Eve.* Don't he have a tree to trim or some goddamn thing? Talk about a shark.

FROGGY: He prolly knew he'd catch you at home. Wrappin presents or somethin.

BAYLIS: The motherfucker put his hands on me first. I was just defendin myself.

FROGGY: You should pay him, Baylis. Just give him a hundred bucks or somethin.

BAYLIS: I don't even have a hundred bucks, Froggy. I just spent half my nut on your bus ticket. I don't care what that lawyer says. *(To the phone)* Fuckin gold-throated sissy!

FROGGY: He said he's gonna call back.

BAYLIS: Good. Let him. *(He takes a dangerous amount of aspirin, chases with whiskey.)*

FROGGY: What was Port Authority like?

BAYLIS: Sad as a goddamn funeral. No, fuck that, that shit was *sadder* than a funeral. Everyone just sittin around waitin. Lookin like a bunch of refugees in some government line. After I take you there tomorrow, I ain't never goin there again. Even if I gotta take a *bus* I ain't goin there. I'll take the Path Train to fuckin Journal Square and get one outta New Jersey. Port Authority's too goddamn depressing for me.

FROGGY: You see Pinchback?

BAYLIS: Yeah, I saw that desperate sonuvabitch.

FROGGY: Did he ask about me?

BAYLIS: Nope.

FROGGY: Fuckin doublejonted H I V zitface.

BAYLIS: Froggy, Pinchback don't give two shits about you. You gotta let that vulturous bastard go. You're lucky he didn't wind up murderin you.

FROGGY: He owes me some heroin. I did him a favor.
He owes me.

BAYLIS: Yeah, what you do, fold his fuckin laundry?
Re-arrange his goddamn stamp collection? You prolly
sucked off one of his slew-footed friends.

(FROGGY *gives him the finger.*)

BAYLIS: I don't know how you let yourself get mixed
up with a dealer in the first place. And a lowlife Port
Authority dealer at that. Hangin out in the bathroom
all day tappin out codes.

(BAYLIS *turns the radio on. A cheerful Christmas choir. They
listen in silence for a moment.* BAYLIS *turns the radio off.*)

FROGGY: Why'd you turn it off?

BAYLIS: Too goddamn cheerful for me.

FROGGY: I liked it. All those little kids.

BAYLIS: Buncha delinquents.

FROGGY: You should come lay down.

BAYLIS: No.

FROGGY: Why not?

BAYLIS: I'm afraid if I lay down I won't be able to get
back up, and then I won't be able to take you to the bus
tomorrow.

FROGGY: So put me in a cab.

BAYLIS: Oh no. You think I'm fuckin stupid? I'm puttin
you on that bus and I ain't leavin till I see it pull away
with your face in the window.

FROGGY: I said I ain't goin nowhere.

BAYLIS: You're goin, Froggy, and that's that! I can't take
care of you. I don't even know what to do.

FROGGY: You don't gotta do nothin. The doctor said there ain't nothin *to* do but rest and wait for the yellow to go away. I'll just stay in bed and stuff.

BAYLIS: Oh yeah, and where am I gonna sleep?

FROGGY: In the bed with me.

BAYLIS: I think hepatitis is contagious, Froggy.

FROGGY: So I won't touch you.

BAYLIS: What if you start sweatin or somethin?

FROGGY: I won't sweat.

BAYLIS: You're sweatin right now. I prolly already got the shit. And now the goddamn window's busted. We'll get frostbite. Fuckin freeze to death... You're burnin up. You swallow those vitamins?

(FROGGY sticks her tongue out, revealing the two, half-melted vitamins.)

BAYLIS: Swallow em.

(She drinks from the water jug, swallows, then sits up.)

FROGGY: I had this dream, Baylis. I was a lion. I was made of snow. I was a snowlion. There was this goat. It was little. Like a baby goat. I was gonna eat it but I started meltin all over the place. I tried to roar but when I opened my mouth that bird flew out—that bird from the window.
   And then you came over on this horse. You were like nine feet tall. You wanted to stop me from meltin and stuff but you couldn't get down from your horse cause you kept poopin your pants.

BAYLIS: What happened to the goat?

FROGGY: I think it turned into a mailman or somethin.

BAYLIS: Was I wearin a diaper?

FROGGY: You were naked.

BAYLIS: How the hell could I crap my pants if I was naked?

FROGGY: I guess you pooped your horse then.

BAYLIS: That's one of them smack dreams. Makes too much fuckin sense to be a regular dream.

(The phone rings. BAYLIS quickly answers.)

BAYLIS: Quit callin here! I said I ain't payin shit you fuckin lowlife shark!...
   Oh, hey, Murl... Sorry, man, I thought you were someone else... Yeah... Uh-huh... Really... No shit... Okay... Okay...
   You gave her the number?... Okay, thanks, Murl. Later... *(He hangs up.)*

FROGGY: What'd Murl want?

BAYLIS: He said your mother called. I guess she called him back after he talked to your father. Murl gave her my number.

FROGGY: She's gonna call here?

BAYLIS: That's what Murl said. You gonna talk to her?

FROGGY: I guess.

BAYLIS: Really.

FROGGY: Uh-huh.

BAYLIS: And you'll tell her what's goin on?

FROGGY: Sure, why not?

BAYLIS: Froggy, what you need to do when you get back to Detroit is get clean. Kick this heroin shit. Get on a methadone program somewhere.

FROGGY: Methadone's for junkies. I ain't no junky.

BAYLIS: Oh, no? What are you, a chemist?

FROGGY: I don't shoot the stuff. I never shoot it.

BAYLIS: Another two weeks you'll be spikin the shit.
Believe me, Froggy, I know, I've been there. When I was
in San Francisco that China White turned to Blackfoot
faster than February. Before you know it you're cookin
it over a fuckin Bunsen burner. Burnt spoons spinnin all
over the place. Wakin up with em in the bed.
   Started out snortin it just like you. Stole shit. Broke
into apartments. Told more lies than Lucifer. Month
and a half later I was skin-poppin and then I was spikin
it. When I moved out here, if it wasn't for Murl gettin
me on that methadone program I'd be fuckin dead,
trust me.

FROGGY: I hear that stuff tastes nasty.

BAYLIS: So it's a little sour. They mix it with Tang.
Tastes like bug juice. Besides you said your dad's a
doctor, right?

FROGGY: Uh-huh.

BAYLIS: What kinda doctor is he?

FROGGY: I don't know. Hearts, I think. He like takes em
out and puts em back in. Cleans em or somethin.

BAYLIS: He'll prolly know about a methadone program
somewhere. There's a clinic in every city. He'll be able
to take good care of you. Drink some more water.

*(The phone rings twice. BAYLIS looks to FROGGY. She nods.
He answers it.)*

BAYLIS: Hello... Beth? ...Oh, hey... Yeah, she's here.
Sure, just a sec...

*(FROGGY rises off the bed, crosses to the desk, takes the
phone. BAYLIS crosses to the window with his cigarette
and whiskey, offering privacy. FROGGY takes the phone
downstage right, near the entrance.)*

FROGGY: Hello?... Hey... Good... New York... New York
City... I don't know, a while...

Just this guy I met...Baylis... *(Looking at* BAYLIS, *no bullshit)* We're gonna have a baby.
I don't know, a few weeks maybe.... I just started pukin and stuff.... Uh-huh...
    Yeah, I got money. Not a lot. I live in New York, you know? The Big Nasty Apple...
    I'm sick... Hepatitis... Uh-huh... I don't know. My arms are yellow and I got a fever.... Yeah, the doctor says it ain't good for the baby... Vitamins. B and C and stuff...
So can I come home?... Well, Baylis bought me a bus ticket....
    I don't know... Okay... Okay...
    Does my room still got a bed in it? ...Uh-huh ...Uh-huh...
You guys got a tree?... Is it real or fake?... Does that kid with the lizards still live across the street?... He did? Okay... Okay... Me, too...
    So I'll call when my bus gets in... Hang on...

*(*BAYLIS *crosses to her the bus ticket, points to a spot, sits at the far edge of the desk.)*

FROGGY: Tomorrow. Just after midnight....
    Yeah, I still look the same, except I'm turnin yellow. Just look for the yellow girl... Okay... Me too...
(She hangs up.)

BAYLIS: Beth, huh?

*(*FROGGY *crosses back to the desk with the phone, sets it down).*

BAYLIS: Nice to meet you, Beth Cunningham.

FROGGY: *(Crossing back to bed)* It's Elizabeth. Elizabeth Ann.

BAYLIS: Good Christian name... Don't worry, I like Froggy better.

FROGGY: What's your name?

BAYLIS: Baylis.

FROGGY: Your real name.

BAYLIS: Baylis is real.

FROGGY: Your first name, Fuckface.

BAYLIS: Eric.

FROGGY: *Eric?*

BAYLIS: Yeah, what's wrong with that?

FROGGY: *(Crossing back to the bed)* Nothin. I like it.
I went to grade school with this kid named Eric.
We called him earache. He used to poop his pants, too.

BAYLIS: Your mom sounded rich. What does she do?

FROGGY: I don't know. Buys stuff. Furniture. Fancy
shoes.

BAYLIS: She look like you?

FROGGY: She's uglier.

BAYLIS: She got red hair, too?

FROGGY: Yeah.

BAYLIS: Gray-green eyes?

FROGGY: Gray. Why?

BAYLIS: I guess I picture her lookin like you. But with a
fur.

FROGGY: She's got a bigger ass. Better skin.

BAYLIS: I'll bet she don't smoke. I'll bet her teeth are
whiter than Park Avenue. She drives a Caddy and the
back seat prolly smells like roses.

FROGGY: She drives a Saab. Her tits are fake and she
chews sugarless gum. She has an account with Laura
Ashley.

BAYLIS: Who the fuck is Lorna Oshlog?

FROGGY: Some prissy designer chick. Curtains and pillowcases and stuff.

BAYLIS: So why'd you leave?

FROGGY: Cause I got pregnant.

BAYLIS: Post-pubescently parturient.

FROGGY: What's that?

BAYLIS: Somethin my mom used to say. She'd see some young girl at the grocery store with a belly out to here and say it. Post-pubescently parturient.

FROGGY: What does parturient mean?

BAYLIS: Parturient: P-A-R-T-U-R-I-E-N-T. *(Shooting her a look)* It means 'bringing forth or about to bring forth young.'

(From her golf bag, FROGGY removes an old Babywipes box. She opens it. It contains makeup. She starts to apply it over the following section. She uses eyeliner, eye shadow, lipstick, mascara.)

FROGGY: Was your mom like a teacher or a something?

BAYLIS: She was a prison nurse. She just liked words. In our house we had more dictionaries than pots and pans. Funny thing is I still grew up a fuckin halfwit. I could spell a dozen ten-dollar words but I couldn't pass grammar if it was taught in a phone booth. Verbs kicked my ass. Prepositions, shit like that.

FROGGY: I had a friend named Verb back in Detroit. He was this kid who used to grow his own weed under science lamps and stuff. Verb Johnson.

BAYLIS: So what happened to the baby?

FROGGY: I was gonna have it but I kept seein it comin out as a bug. Like a roach or a spider or somethin.

BAYLIS: You got an abortion?

FROGGY: Sort of. I went to this guy my dealer knew.

BAYLIS: Jesus Christ, Froggy, you were doin fuckin smack in high school?

FROGGY: Mostly just coke and weed. Crystal meth. Smoked crack a coupla times, too.

BAYLIS: Janice fuckin Joplin.

FROGGY: I used to put heroin on the end of a cigarette. It's really good that way. Gets all in your lungs and stuff.

BAYLIS: So what did this guy do - this friend of your dealer's?

FROGGY: He would like give these abortions that weren't really abortions. They weren't like done in a hospital or a clinic.

BAYLIS: Where were they done, at the grocery store?

FROGGY: In this garage with carparts and stuff. You wait in this alley next to a payphone. When it rings twice this door opens and you go in the garage and this guy feels you. Like your stomach and your pussy and stuff. And then you drink this blue crap that tastes like puke and stand in this metal bucket thing and he starts hitting you in the stomach with a hammer until it starts comin out.

BAYLIS: What starts comin out—the blue shit?

FROGGY: Hunks of stuff. I kept expecting to see babyparts. Like a little hand or a foot. But the only thing that kept comin out were these bloody pieces of meat. Like meat from the deli. Ham or baloney or somethin.

BAYLIS: Did it hurt?

FROGGY: Sort of, but I did some mescaline so it wasn't too bad. I couldn't walk too good afterwards. I was gonna take a cab to my dealer's house but the guy from the garage took all my money. He was supposed to take a hundred, but he took forty more cause I puked on him. So I took the bus back instead.

BAYLIS: What about the father?

FROGGY: What about him?

BAYLIS: Didn't he help you?

FROGGY: No.

BAYLIS: Why not?

FROGGY: He didn't even know.

BAYLIS: You never told him?

FROGGY: Nu-uh.

BAYLIS: Who was he?

FROGGY: He was my dad.

BAYLIS: Your *dad.*

(FROGGY *nods.*)

BAYLIS: Your dad, the Doctor?

FROGGY: Uh-huh.

BAYLIS: Your dad the fucking golfing heart surgeon?

(FROGGY *finishes with her makeup and hair, rises out of bed, crosses to the window, looks out.*)

FROGGY: We screwed for like a month. He had a small dick but it wasn't bad... Hey, Baylis, was Pinchback wearin a corduroy coat?

BAYLIS: I don't know.

FROGGY: He said he was gonna gimme that coat.

BAYLIS: Enough about Pinchback, okay?

(FROGGY *cries out suddenly, clutching her side, doubles over, almost falls.* BAYLIS *moves to her as quickly as possible,*

helps her back to the bed. She cries out again. It's bad.
BAYLIS *doesn't know what to do. They are quiet in the*
bed for a long moment.)

BAYLIS: Froggy, why didn't you tell me about all that.
About your dad?

*(*FROGGY *doesn't answer.)*

BAYLIS: Well, fuck.

FROGGY: What.

BAYLIS: Nothin. *(He crosses back to the desk, sets the chair a*
little closer to the bed, sits.)

FROGGY: Hey, Baylis.

BAYLIS: What.

FROGGY: How old was your mom when she croaked?

BAYLIS: I don't know. Forty-two, forty-three.

FROGGY: Was she murdered?

BAYLIS: She died of cancer.

FROGGY: Were you with her?

BAYLIS: Yeah, I was with her.

FROGGY: Did she like give a speech or somethin?

BAYLIS: No, Froggy, she didn't give a speech.

FROGGY: Did she cry and stuff?

BAYLIS: She just sorta went to sleep. Before she faded
she kept talkin about how she couldn't feel her legs.
But they had the morphine drip goin, so she wasn't too
scared. And she couldn't see too good either, but that's
it. You seen too many movies.

FROGGY: What about your dad?

BAYLIS: He was a diabetic. He had a heart attack.
I wasn't around when he died.

FROGGY: Where were you?

BAYLIS: On my way home from Iraq.

FROGGY: If my parents died I wouldn't care. But if they were murdered I'd be pissed. Like if they got their heads chopped off or somethin.

BAYLIS: Before you said once you're croaked you're croaked.

FROGGY: I know, but I want them to live a long time so their bodies break down. So their bones rot with poison and stuff. Then they'll feel the pain for like forty years. Gettin murdered would be too easy. Like shootin a dog or somethin.

BAYLIS: I spose that makes some kinda sense.

FROGGY: You know what's weird, Baylis?

BAYLIS: What.

FROGGY: I can't feel my legs too good.

BAYLIS: You jokin?

(She shakes her head.)

BAYLIS: You want me to rub em?

FROGGY: Yeah, but let me put my head in your armpit first.

BAYLIS: I prolly smell like a wet bull.

FROGGY: You smell like the bottom of a popcorn box.

BAYLIS: I do?

FROGGY: Uh-huh. It's nice. It's like bein at the movies.

(He crosses to the bed, sits, and lets her nestle her head in his armpit.)

FROGGY: *(Nestling)* I'm like a puppy.

(After a moment, he leans over her legs, rubs them for a moment, notices the picture she's been drawing.)

BAYLIS: Whatchu been drawin?

(She shows him. It's a picture of a blackbird. He stares at it a moment.)

BAYLIS: Fuckin art, huh?

(She hides it under the covers.)

FROGGY: Hey, Baylis.

BAYLIS: Hey, Froggy.

FROGGY: You shot at people in that war, right?

BAYLIS: Yeah, I shot at people.

FROGGY: When you felt the gun go off, did you get a boner?

BAYLIS: No, why?

FROGGY: Cause Pinchback told me he shot a gun once and it gave him a boner.

BAYLIS: That's what happens when you mix guns and derelicts.

FROGGY: Murl's got a gun, right?

BAYLIS: Yeah, Froggy, he's got a gun.

FROGGY: Maybe you could like borrow it. Take it up to the roof and just shoot it a few times.

(BAYLIS crosses back to his chair. FROGGY turns over the piece of paper that she's been drawing on. She starts to read text from it aloud.)

FROGGY: He goes in the bathroom. Slams the door. Ahhh! He rips the shower curtain open. Baby, you scare me. Laughter. Good times. Take your clothes off, Little Pony. Giggles. They make love. It's intense, physical shower sex.

BAYLIS: Where'd you get that?

FROGGY: Hang on. *(Reading again)* Later. Baby you fucked the shit out of me. I'm sore. He giggles. Chuckles a bit. I'M FUCKIN SORE MY PUSSY'S BURNIN.

BAYLIS: HEY!

FROGGY: Little Pony, I don't have any money. Baby, I'm brome... What's brome?

(BAYLIS crosses to her as quickly as he can, snatches the papers away.)

BAYLIS: It's sposed to say broke. *Broke.* Not fucking *brome.* It's a typo.

FROGGY: What is that?

BAYLIS: Somethin I was writin. It's a movie. A love story. It's sposed to be intimate. Like in a sexy way.

FROGGY: It sounds like a porno.

BAYLIS: Well, it's not.

FROGGY: MY PUSSY'S BURNIN?!

BAYLIS: There's this whole other part where they go into the woods and find a bird. Like a dove. It's dead. They put it in a box and bury it. It's like a metaphor or a theme or some shit. They find it during the magic hour.

FROGGY: Is that like when the unicorns come out or somethin?

BAYLIS: It's dusk, okay? *(He reads the script for a moment.)*

BAYLIS: Did you like it?

FROGGY: Yeah.

BAYLIS: Really?

FROGGY: I like how they talk and stuff. How he keeps calling her Little Pony.

BAYLIS: It's masculine, right?

FROGGY: You should like make a video or somethin.

BAYLIS: You think?

FROGGY: It's good stuff, Baylis.

BAYLIS: Thanks, Froggy.

(The phone rings. He answers it.)

BAYLIS: Hello... Yeah, that's me.... Uh-huh... You like harassin people, don't you? You don't got nothin better to do on Christmas Eve?... Uh-huh... Uh-huh... Really... Jesus... Yeah, I heard you... Okay... Okay... *(He hangs up, stands very still, unplugs the phone line.)*

FROGGY: That lawyer?

BAYLIS: Yeah.

FROGGY: What'd he say?

BAYLIS: He said that that guy I hit needs seventeen thousand dollars worth of reconstructive surgery on his forehead. And that he's havin trouble speakin.

FROGGY: How many times did you hit him, Baylis?

BAYLIS: I don't remember. More than once maybe. The lawyer said he might have brain damage.

FROGGY: But he hit you first, right?

BAYLIS: I don't know, Froggy. I thought he did.... *(He crosses to the window, stares out, dejected.)*

FROGGY: I hit this little kid with my lunchbox once. At the bus-stop. He kept grabbin my tit so I swung at him. Hit him right in the face, too. He was a only a sixth grader. His mouth was all bloody and stuff but I didn't care. Taught him a lesson... What are you lookin at?

BAYLIS: I don't know. Nothin. Everyone's out there tryin to beat Christmas. Runnin around like the fuckin flood's comin. Don't make any damn sense to me.

FROGGY: Hey, Baylis.

BAYLIS: Huh.

FROGGY: Are you still gonna make me get on that bus tomorrow?

BAYLIS: I don't know. Maybe. I ain't too thrilled about the idea of harboring a girl with someone else's baby. I know it ain't mine... Is it Murl's?... Is it?

FROGGY: I'll go if you want me to. I'll look at you through the window and stuff. I'll watch you till you disappear.
   You could do all kinds of stuff without me. No Froggy the Frog getting in the way.
   But if I stay you'll get to make me rest and stuff. Take my temperature. Tell me what to do. It'll be fun, right?

BAYLIS: Sure, Froggy. It'll be fun.

FROGGY: We can pretend it's your baby.

(A pecking at the window)

FROGGY: The bird again?

BAYLIS: Uh-huh.

FROGGY: What's it doin?

BAYLIS: Nothin. Just starin back at me.

FROGGY: *(Out)* Can you see its tongue?

BAYLIS: Uh-huh.

FROGGY: *(Out)* It's blue, right?

BAYLIS: Yeah, it is blue. *(He crosses to the closet, removes a kit containing a syringe and a rubber tube, crosses to the desk with his works, sits. From the pocket of his housecoat he*

*removes the vial of Novocain, draws the liquid into the
syringe, prepares the tourniquet, and mainlines the Novocain
over the following.)*

FROGGY: Hey, Baylis.

BAYLIS: Hey, Froggy

FROGGY: You know that code I was tappin earlier?

BAYLIS: Uh-huh.

FROGGY: One-four-three. It was special.

BAYLIS: I know, Froggy. I know.

FROGGY: It was for you, Baylis. One-four-three.

BAYLIS: One-four-three, right back at you, Froggy.
One-four-three.

*(When BAYLIS is finished, he starts to prod his hand, his
arms, his stomach. Through the window we can see that it
has started to snow.)*

FROGGY: Did you turn the light off or somethin?

BAYLIS: No, Froggy. The light's still on.

FROGGY: You sure?

BAYLIS: Yeah, I'm sure.

FROGGY: It's gettin darker in here. Like clouds and stuff.

BAYLIS: It's snowin.

FROGGY: I'm cold.

BAYLIS: Yeah, me too. I'm cold, too. *(He crosses to the
entrance, grabs his coat.)* I'm gonna turn the light off now,
okay?

FROGGY: Uh-huh.

*(BAYLIS crosses to the futon covers her with his leather
jacket, gets in next to her, using his body to keep her warm,
protecting her from the window. He puts her hat back on.)*

FROGGY: Is the window busted bad?

BAYLIS: Yeah, pretty bad.

FROGGY: Is the bird still there?

BAYLIS: He's still there.

FROGGY: I can't feel my legs.

BAYLIS: Sshshssh.

FROGGY: It's like they went away.

BAYLIS: Just go to sleep.

FROGGY: Okay.

BAYLIS: I'm right here.

FROGGY: Everything's all squiggly and stuff.

BAYLIS: I know.

FROGGY: That's okay, right? Little squiggles?

BAYLIS: Everything's gonna be okay.

FROGGY: It's okay, cause I'm a lion right?

BAYLIS: You're a lion, Froggy.

FROGGY: I think I'm snowin, Baylis. *(She holds her hand out, wiggling her fingers as if it's snow falling.)* Baylis, I'm snowin.

(Her hand descends into his. Lights fade on the room. Cat Power's cover of I Found A Reason *plays as lights fade. Only the blinking light on the window as the snow continues to fall.)*

END OF PLAY